The Scatterbrained Scarecrow of Oz

A play

Alfred Bradley

Samuel French – London
New York – Sydney – Toronto – Hollywood

CHARACTERS

Aunt Em
Uncle Henry
Dorothy
The Guardian of the Gates of Oz
The Fieldmouse
The Witch's Cat
The Wicked Witch of the North
Brat, her goblin son
The Cowardly Lion
The Scarecrow
The Tinman
Glinda, the Good Witch of the South
The Black Spirit
The Music Man
Kay, the Queen of the Kaleidoscope
The Wizard of Oz

Dorothy, the Scarecrow, the Cowardly Lion and the Tinman go all through the story. The other parts may be doubled so that it is possible to stage the play with nine actors

AUTHOR'S NOTES

The Scatterbrained Scarecrow of Oz is a sequel to *The Wizard of Oz* and Dorothy, the Scarecrow, the Cowardly Lion and the Tinman are based on the characters immortalized in L. Frank Baum's classic American children's novel. The fact that the original story was set in Kansas has been ignored as the characters don't need to belong to any particular country and for many actors an American accent is not easy to come by.

This version of the play can be produced very simply, it needs no stage and may be performed in the round on the floor of a school hall. There is, of course, nothing to prevent a more ambitious production using back-projection, flash-boxes and all of the other magic which a proscenium theatre can provide but it is essential to keep the settings simple; this is the story of a journey and heavy sets of the Victorian toy-theatre sort will tend to hold up the action. It is useful to have the playing area broken up into a number of different levels and if these are planned to serve as the table, the Witch's stove and the Wizard's chest, scene shifting will be cut to a minimum. If the rostra are painted in a neutral colour, lighting changes will produce strong contrasts which will add interest to the journey and imaginative use of light will provide the wall, the kaleidoscope and increase the effect of the Witch's spells.

With a simplified setting, sound becomes very important: some of the effects like the whirlwind will need to be pre-recorded but a percussionist equipped with a wide range of accessories will emphasize the fun of the Scarecrow's falls, help the actors to move from one scene to another and generally add to the excitement.

The costumes should present no difficulty but it is a good idea to prepare the Tinman's suit well in advance so that it can be worn at rehearsals. Aunt Em and Uncle Henry are best dressed in grey or brown to contrast with the colourful world of Dorothy's imagination. Masks tend to muffle voices and, after the initial effect has worn off, leave the actors with little expression, so it is preferable to use bold character make-up for the Scarecrow, the Lion and the Tinman.

As yet, we have very few theatres which regularly present plays for children and it is not really surprising that actors coming across boldly drawn characters for the first time may be inclined to send them up and to add adult references to the script. Any temptation to guy the characters must be resisted; jokes and inconsistencies which a young audience cannot be expected to understand are a luxury which we cannot afford. The audience will only believe in the people in the story if we believe in them ourselves.

ACT I

The farm where Dorothy lives with her aunt and uncle. It is evening

Uncle Henry is trimming the lamp and Aunt Em is knitting busily

Em Put the lamp here, Henry, then I can see better.

Henry Right. (*He moves the lamp across the table*) What are you making, Em?

Em A thick pair of socks for Dorothy. That child is always running around without her shoes. If she has some new socks, her feet will be warm at least.

Henry I thought she already had some warm socks.

Em She had. I've never known a child like her for losing things. She couldn't find her coat yesterday. She searched through every cupboard in the house.

Henry And where was it?

Em She had it on all the time.

Dorothy hurries in

Dorothy Aunt Em, have you seen Toto?

Em Not since I saw you talking to him in the farmyard this morning.

Henry Have you looked everywhere?

Dorothy Yes, everywhere!

Henry In your pinafore pocket?

Dorothy Of course! (*But she looks in her pocket just to be sure and finds her pet mouse*) Toto, there you are! Wherever have you been?

Henry (*chuckling*) What did I tell you? I expect he's been worried.

Dorothy Worried?

Henry The sky has been very dark all day.

Em I thought we were in for a storm.

Dorothy He doesn't like storms.

Henry And nor do I. The last one was enough for one lifetime.

Em Don't remind me. It lifted this house into the air as if it was paper. And it's taken us over a year to rebuild it. I never want to see another like that.

Dorothy I know it was terrible and very frightening at first, but I'll always remember it because it blew me away above the clouds and into the Wonderful Land of Oz.

Em Your imagination child! Sometimes I think you live most of your life in dreams.

Dorothy It wasn't a dream, Aunt Em, I'm sure it wasn't. I met some very strange people, but they were real, I know they were. A scarecrow, a lion and a tinman . . .

Henry Anyway, I hope we don't get another like it. It was worse than a storm. More like a cyclone.

Dorothy A cyclone?

Henry Yes, that's what they called it. A great whirlwind which snapped great trees and crushed houses like matchboxes. It's lucky that we had the cellar to hide in.

Dorothy It's hard to believe that a wind could be as powerful as that but it must have been if it blew me all the way to the Land of Oz.

Henry (*peering into the sky*) I don't like the look of it.

Em Henry, I think you ought to lock the chickens up. Those clouds look very threatening to me.

Henry All right, I'll do it now.

Dorothy I'll come with you. (*She peers into her pocket*) Come along Toto, we'll help Uncle Henry with the chickens. Don't worry, you'll be quite safe in there.

Em Don't be long.

Dorothy We won't.

She follows Henry off

Em tidies away her knitting and clears the table

Em (*worried*) I don't like it at all.

The sky darkens. A clap of thunder very close. A sudden rush of wind

Henry, Dorothy, come back here quickly! It's another cyclone! It's just like last time! Quickly! Oh . . . please hurry! (*She hurries towards the cellar*) Henry! (*She opens the trapdoor and begins to go down the steps*) Quickly, we'll be safe down here!

Henry enters

Henry (*battling against the wind*) Dorothy! Where are you?

Dorothy enters

Dorothy Here! I'm over here! I can't find Toto!

Henry Don't worry about him. We must get to the cellar.

Dorothy I can't leave him behind. He's afraid of thunder. I must find him. You go in.

Henry Come along. He can look after himself. Dorothy!

There is no answer

He gives up and goes down the cellar steps

Dorothy Toto, please come back Toto, the thunder won't hurt you. You must come back. I can't go without you.

The wind rises to a crescendo, spinning her like a top

Toto!

The furniture drifts away

Oh dear! Here we go again.

A crack of lightning and a crash of thunder

Toto! Toto! (*And she goes on calling to him as she is carried further and further away. It is now completely dark*)

Strange music. When the Light returns, Dorothy is lying on the ground. The wind has dropped her in front of the great ornamental gates of the Palace of Oz

Wherever am I? Uncle Henry, Aunt Em, where are you? (*She finds Toto in her pocket*) Toto! There you are! In my pocket all the time. Where can we be? We must have come a very long way from home. And do you know, I've lost my shoes.

The Guardian of the gates of Oz appears. He is strutting up and down on sentry duty and doesn't see Dorothy for a moment

Excuse me. Haven't we met before somewhere?

Guardian I don't think so. (*He continues marching*)

Dorothy I'm sure your face is familiar.

Guardian And so are you. Too familiar. Don't you understand, you're not supposed to talk to a sentry when he's on duty.

Dorothy (*going up to him*) Are you on duty?

Guardian Of course I am! Do you think I stamp up and down like this at home?

Dorothy I don't expect so. It would wear out the carpet.

Guardian There you are then.

Dorothy (*following behind him as he marches up and down*) Can you tell me where I am?

Guardian It's obvious, isn't it?

Dorothy Not really.

Guardian What colour is the sky?

Dorothy That's a funny question. Green.

Guardian And what colour is it where you come from?

Dorothy Well it's sometimes blue and sometimes grey. Today it was nearly black.

Guardian Blue, grey or black?

Dorothy Yes.

Guardian But never green?

Dorothy That's right. I wish you would stop marching!

Guardian Very well. (*He stamps to a halt*) Now there's only one place where the sky is green.

Dorothy Of course. The Land of Oz.

Guardian That's right. And that's where you are.

Dorothy I knew I'd seen you before somewhere! You were guarding the gates when I came before.

Guardian Before?

Dorothy Yes, when I came to see the Wizard with the Scarecrow.

Guardian The Scarecrow! You know the Scarecrow?

Dorothy Of course, don't you remember?

Guardian I'm getting old. My memory isn't what it was ... yes, now I come to think hard I do remember, you had some strange friends with you, a lion and a man made of tin.

Dorothy That's right, the Cowardly Lion and the Tin Woodman.

Guardian Well, it's nice to have met you again, but you must go away now and let me get on with my job.

Dorothy What is your job?

Guardian To stop people like you from bothering the ruler of the Land of Oz.

Dorothy But who is the ruler of Oz?

Guardian It used to be a Wizard—but he sailed away in a hot air balloon. Now we are ruled by the Scarecrow.

Dorothy Of course! The Wizard put him in charge when he decided to go back home. The Scarecrow is one of my oldest friends. When can I see him?

Guardian I don't know that you *can* see him. He used to see everybody who called but just lately he has shut himself away in his throne room and refused to meet anybody.

Dorothy Will you please tell him that I'm here?

Guardian It won't do any good.

Dorothy Please!

Guardian (*after a moment's thought*) Very well, but I don't think you'll be lucky. What is your name?

Dorothy Just tell him it's Dorothy and Toto.

Guardian Dorothy Anne who?

Dorothy No. My name is Dorothy, and this is my pet mouse, Toto. (*She shows Toto to him*)

Guardian I shouldn't leave my post, you know, it's most irregular. If the Captain of the Guard appears, I'll get into terrible trouble.

Dorothy (*pleading*) It won't take a minute.

Guardian All right. Now I come to think of it, I do remember your mouse. Hello Toto.

He salutes and after some elaborate about-turning marches off

Dorothy (*to Toto*) I didn't think we would get to the Palace of Oz so quickly. Last time there was a cyclone it took days and days. I wonder if the Scarecrow has forgotten me? I expect he has lots of things on his mind nowadays. He must be very clever to be ruler of the Land of Oz. I don't expect he'll remember anybody unimportant like me.

The Guardian strides back in and comes to a smart halt

Guardian I have spoken to the great Scarecrow of Oz. He has graciously consented to grant you an audience.

Dorothy Thank you.

A cymbal clash. The gates open and we see the Scarecrow who is seated upon an emerald throne. He wears a golden crown round the brim of his battered old felt hat

Dorothy drops him a curtsy

Your Majesty, it is very kind of you to agree to see me.

Scarecrow (*standing up amazed*) Dorothy! Can it really be you? (*He comes down and lifts her to her feet*) My dear friend, I can hardly believe my eyes.

Dorothy Oh, Scarecrow, it is good to see you. (*She hugs him for a moment*)

Scarecrow And I can't tell you how pleased I am to see you. But how did you get here?

Dorothy Oh, it's a long story, a great wind carried me away above the clouds and dropped me here. But tell me about yourself. Are you enjoying being the King of the Land of Oz?

Scarecrow I was until about three days ago when a very strange thing happened ... (*He realizes that the Guardian is still there and full of curiosity*) Thank you, Guardian, you may go now.

Guardian Are you sure you wouldn't like me to stay here in case you want anything?

Scarecrow No, I'll send for you if I need you.

Guardian All right. (*As he goes*) Just when the conversation was getting interesting ...

The Guardian goes

Scarecrow It's very important that nobody else should hear. Are you listening?

Dorothy Yes.

Scarecrow Good. When we met before and went to see the Wizard of Oz, do you remember what he gave me?

Dorothy Of course I do. You wanted a brain so that you would be clever and he gave you one. It was a little pin-cushion full of pins and needles.

Scarecrow That's right. And when he put it inside my hat, it made me feel very sharp. Later on, when he decided to sail away in his balloon, he said that I was the cleverest man in the whole of Oz and made me the ruler of the Emerald City.

Dorothy I remember.

Scarecrow My people gave me this crown and I felt very proud. I didn't want my new brains to get rusty so I used them hard and tried my best to make the Land of Oz a happy place for everybody. But now ...

Dorothy What's happened, Scarecrow?

Scarecrow Are you sure that nobody's listening? (*He peers round*) Come here.

She comes closer

I've lost them.

Dorothy But that's impossible. I often lose things, I know, but you can't lose your brains.

Scarecrow Look. (*He takes off his crown and his felt hat. He taps his head which produces a solid knocking sound*) Empty! I'm brainless again.

Dorothy It's upsetting, I can see that. But never mind, Scarecrow. I liked you before you had any brains so it doesn't make any difference.

Scarecrow But I must have brains if I am to be a wise ruler. Who could have taken them? Do you think it was a witch?

Dorothy I don't think that there are any witches left in Oz. The wicked witches who lived in the East and West and South are dead. And we know that the Witch of the North is a good witch because she helped us before.

Scarecrow Then who could it be?

Dorothy I don't know.

A Fieldmouse rushes in pursued by a Cat who chases her in all directions. Suddenly the Cat finds himself face to face with the Scarecrow who raises his arms and shouts "Boo!" The Cat gives a loud shriek and rushes off

Fieldmouse Oh, thank you. I thought that was the end of me. I'm not usually afraid of cats but that cat belongs to a witch.

Dorothy But aren't all the witches dead?

Fieldmouse All but the Witch of the North.

Dorothy But surely she's a good witch?

Fieldmouse The Witch of the North used to be a good witch but she became jealous of Glinda the good witch who helps everybody and tried to put a spell on her. It went wrong and turned the Witch of the North into somebody evil. Now she is even uglier than the wicked witches who used to rule this land. You have been very kind to me so I will tell you a secret.

Scarecrow Oh good. I like secrets!

Fieldmouse I heard the Witch of the North talking to the goblin she calls her son. She was plotting to steal some brains.

Scarecrow Just as I thought.

Dorothy But what would she want them for?

Fieldmouse I don't know. A spell maybe.

Dorothy We must find her. Where does she live?

Fieldmouse In a castle in the Mountains of Darkness which lie to the North of Oz.

Dorothy Then we must go there at once.

Fieldmouse I'm sure you are very brave but it is a long way to the Witch's castle and she has evil powers which will make the journey dangerous.

Dorothy It's a risk that we will have to take.

Fieldmouse I see that your mind is made up. But you would be sensible to take somebody strong with you.

Scarecrow I know. Why don't we go and ask our friend the Lion to help? Maybe he will come with us. He is the most courageous beast in the forest.

Dorothy That's a good idea. And I'd like to see the Lion again.

Scarecrow That's settled then.

Fieldmouse Thank you again for helping me. Take this with you.

Scarecrow What is it?

Fieldmouse A whistle.

Scarecrow (*blowing it*) So it is.

Fieldmouse A magic whistle. If you are ever in trouble, blow it and I will come.

Scarecrow I don't want to sound rude, but how could a little mouse help us?

Fieldmouse I may seem a little mouse to you, but I am a queen. The Queen of all the Fieldmice. And although we are very small, there are thousands of us so we may be able to help more than you think.

Scarecrow You'll certainly be able to do that. I can't think at all!

Fieldmouse Don't forget. Goodbye.

She goes

Dorothy Goodbye!

Scarecrow Goodbye. Are we ready?

Dorothy Yes, put your crown on again.

Scarecrow All right. (*He does*) But I feel a fraud. Rulers ought to have brains.

Dorothy Well, most of them haven't so I shouldn't let it worry you too much.

Scarecrow I don't know how far it is to the Witch's castle but I can't wait to get there!

They go off

The Lights fade. Eerie music. When it gets lighter we see the Wicked Witch of the North. She is rubbing her hands together with glee. She calls to her goblin son

Witch Brat!

Brat (*not the brightest of boys*) Yes, Mother?

Witch There you are.

Brat Am I? Oh yes, so I am.

Witch Things are working out even better than I expected.

Brat Are they?

Witch Where's that other stupid creature? Cat!

Cat slinks in

Cat Here I am.

Witch (*mocking*) Here I am! Do you know where the Lion lives?

Cat The one who used to be a coward?

Witch That's the one.

Cat They say he has made his home in a cave outside the city in the Hills of the Hammerheads. But nobody goes near him, he's too dangerous. Certainly I've never been there.

Witch Yet!

Cat What do you mean, yet? You're not expecting me to go there are you?

Witch Listen. He isn't really brave but the Wizard of Oz gave him a bottle of courage and as long as he has that, he thinks he is the bravest beast in the forest. He used to be called the Cowardly Lion.

Cat Well, I'm a cowardly cat so that makes two of us.

Witch The Scarecrow and that girl are going to ask him to help them on their journey to my castle.

Cat Why are they going there?

Witch To try to get back the Scarecrow's brains which I stole from the Palace of Oz.

Brat But you've got lots of toads and newts and spiders for your spells, why do you want a poor Scarecrow's brains?

Witch I don't want them for a spell. Without them he can't rule the Land of Oz. I'll let him get to my castle and then I'll throw him into the dungeon. I'll take the crown from him and become the ruler of Oz myself. I will make the people of the Emerald City into my slaves.

Brat I wish you weren't so ambitious.

Witch Don't you want to become a prince?

Brat Can't I just be a goblin like my friends?

Witch No you can't! Now listen, tonight you will go to the Lion's cave with the cat and you will steal the bottle of courage which the Lion keeps there.

Cat But I'm afraid of lions.

Brat I'm afraid of everything.

Witch You'll be more afraid if you don't do as I say. Off you go!

Brat and Cat set off reluctantly

So silly Scarecrow and dear little Dorothy, watch out. Without his courage the Lion won't be able to help as much as you think. (*She chuckles with glee*)

The Witch exits

The Lights fade. When the Light returns we are in a clearing in the wood

A roar and the Lion bounds in. He roars again and then begins to laugh

Lion Oh dear! Sometimes I roar so loud, I frighten myself. I used to be frightened all the time, of course, but since I got my courage I've been the bravest animal in the world. (*He yawns*) Oh! I've had such a good day roaring through the jungle. I don't even have to fight anybody—as soon as they hear me coming they run away. It's a good life being the King of the Beasts. (*He yawns again*) I think I'll have a sleep for a few hours and then in the morning after a swig of courage I'll have another marvellous day's roaring. Now, if I put the bottle down here, I won't forget. I'll keep it near me so that nobody steals it. (*He puts it down beside him*) Oh dear, I'm so tired ... (*He falls asleep*)

As soon as he does so, Brat and Cat appear

Cat I don't like the look of him at all.

Brat Shh! You'll wake him! Go on then!

Cat Right! Go on then, what?

Brat Get the bottle.

Cat You get it.

Brat She told you to get it.

Cat She said we were to get it together.

Brat All right, how shall we do it?

Cat Just sneak up and grab it.

Brat You'd better do it. You'll be quieter than me.

Cat No, I've got an idea. You get it and if he wakes up, I'll draw attention to myself so that he chases me. When you're quite safe, I'll run up a tree where he can't get at me.

Brat (*doubtfully*) I don't like it but here goes.

He tiptoes towards the Lion who stirs in his sleep. He tries again, the Lion snores suddenly. Third time lucky, he gets the bottle

He runs off followed by the Cat

After a moment the Scarecrow and Dorothy come into the clearing and find the Lion asleep

Dorothy There he is! Just as I remember him.

Scarecrow Don't forget that he's a changed character now that he isn't a coward.

Dorothy Would he hurt us?

Scarecrow I don't think so, but you can't be too sure. Shall we wake him?

Dorothy Yes. I think we must.

Scarecrow All right. (*He calls into the Lion's ear*) Lion.

No response

Lion!

The Lion jumps to his feet with his fists up. With one blow he sends the Scarecrow flying and then he turns towards Dorothy

Dorothy Just a moment, friend, don't you recognize us?

Lion Why, it's Dorothy! I never expected to see you again. (*He embraces her*) Have you brought Toto with you?

Dorothy Yes, here he is.

Lion He doesn't grow very much, does he?

Scarecrow Hallo Lion.

Lion Hallo old friend, what are you doing down there? (*He helps the Scarecrow to his feet*) Well, what brings you here?

Scarecrow My legs.

Lion Yes, I know that. I mean why have you come?

Scarecrow Because something terrible has happened.

Lion Go on.

Scarecrow You tell him, Dorothy.

Dorothy The Scarecrow has had his new brains stolen.

Lion Well that doesn't matter does it? I liked him just as much before he got them.

Scarecrow That may be so. But I can't be a king without brains.

Lion (*thoughtfully*) That's true. Kings should be wise. We must do something about it.

Dorothy We know that they were stolen by the Wicked Witch of the North. We are going to seek her out in her castle in the Mountains of Darkness and we thought you might be willing to come along too. We couldn't come to any harm with you beside us.

Lion That's true. Now that I have my courage, I'm not afraid of anybody. Of course I'll come with you. (*A sudden thought*) Where is it?

Scarecrow What?

Lion My courage. It was here when I went to sleep. A big green bottle.

Scarecrow It isn't here now. Who could have taken it? The Witch do you think?

Dorothy Or maybe her Cat.

Lion (*beginning to cry*) Boo hoo!

Dorothy (*consoling him*) There, there. If it was the Witch we'll soon find it. You were coming with us to the castle anyway.

Lion You don't understand. Without my courage I'll be no use to you. I'll just be a coward, afraid of everybody like I was before.

Scarecrow Well, nobody will know that you've lost it so if you roar as usual, they'll run away as usual.

Dorothy That's right. You'll still be useful to us.

Lion Very well. (*He dries his tears with his tail*) But we won't find it easy and the jungle gets very overgrown. You haven't got an axe have you?

Scarecrow No, but I know who has. The Tinman!

Dorothy The Tinman, of course. Oh you are clever, Scarecrow!

The Scarecrow, pleased, looks very coy

But I don't know where he lives.

Scarecrow I do. And it isn't far away. We'll soon get to the Witch's castle with him to help us. Come on, it's a bit dark in the wood, but we'll find him.

Lion I'm afraid of the dark.

Dorothy It's all right Lion, I'll hold your hand.

They go off

As they go, the Lights fade. When the Lights come up again, the Witch is crouched over an evil steaming cauldron

Witch (*mocking*) It's all right Lion, I'll hold your hand. (*She cackles*) Cat! Brat!

They come in

Did you get it?

Brat What?

Witch The Lion's courage, of course.

Brat Yes, here it is. (*He gives it to her*)

Witch Oh you clever boy. Good.

Brat It seemed a pity. He was really rather a pleasant sort of Lion.

Witch Oh you blockhead. With this inside him he could tear us all to pieces. Cat!

Cat Yes.

Witch (*sweetly*) Dear Pussy . . .

Cat Now what are you after?

Witch At the edge of the forest is a cottage. In it lives a woodman made completely out of tin.

Brat Why is he made out of tin?

Witch He was bewitched a long time ago.

Brat Doesn't he mind?

Witch He's got used to it. And since the Wizard of Oz gave him a heart he's been very happy.

Brat Oh good!

Witch It isn't good.

Brat Isn't it? Why?

Witch Because I don't like people to be happy and because he's a friend of the Cowardly Lion and the Scarecrow and that dear little Dorothy.

Brat The ones who are on the way to your castle.

Witch Clever boy! Now, you two are to go to the Tinman and steal his heart.

Cat How can we do that? If he's made of tin we won't be able to get it.

Witch It's very easy. He has a small metal door in his chest. You just open it and take it.

Brat When he is asleep?

Witch No, you stupid brat. Being made of tin he never gets tired like we do so he never goes to sleep. You will have to think of another way to get it.

Brat But I'm not clever at thinking up ways of getting things.

Witch Do as you're told! And you'd better hurry or there'll be trouble.

Cat Oh come on. It's easier to do it than to stand here arguing.

They go

Witch I don't like the attitude of that Cat. (*She cheers up*) Now, I've got the Scarecrow's brains and the Lion's courage. All I need is the Tinman's heart and the crown of Oz will be mine!

The cauldron flares brightly for a moment then the Light fades

When the Lights come up again we are at the edge of the wood. The Cat comes in followed by Brat

Cat This way.

Brat Are you sure?

Cat Yes, I can see his cottage in the distance.

Brat How are we going to get his heart?

Cat I've had an idea. All we need is a bucket of water.

Brat Why? Are you thirsty?

Cat No, of course not! He's made of tin, isn't he?

Brat Yes, we know that.

Cat All we have to do is throw a bucket of water over him. Then, when he's too rusty to move, we'll steal his heart and run away.

Brat It sounds like a nasty trick.

Cat Well, we're nasty people, aren't we?

Brat Sometimes I wish I was a goodie.

Cat With a mother like yours, you haven't a chance. Now I'll talk to him whilst you get a bucket of water from the well. Then you creep up behind him and splash! Right?

Brat All right.

Cat I can see something glinting in the distance. Here he comes. Off you go before he sees you.

Brat goes off

The Tinman comes in carrying his axe and whistling cheerfully

Tinman Oh. Hello.

Cat Good day, Tinman. I don't think we've met before.

Tinman Fancy being able to talk. What a clever cat you are.

Cat Yes, that's true, I am. (*Cunning*) Do you keep your watch behind that little door?

Tinman In here? (*He indicates the door of his chest*) Oh no, I don't use a watch, I never get tired so I don't need to know the time. That's where I keep my heart.

Cat How extraordinary.

Tinman Yes, I suppose it is. I didn't have one for a long time but the kind Wizard of Oz gave me one and it's made me very happy. If you've always had a heart you've no idea how miserable life can be without one.

Brat comes in with the water

Cat Now!

As Brat throws the pail of water, the Tinman bends down to pick something up, the Cat gets soaked

Brat goes off with the bucket

Ow!

Tinman (*standing up again*) Is something the matter?

Cat Oh no!

Tinman (*holding out his hand*) Do you see what this is? It's a little ant. I nearly trod on it. I have to be very careful where I walk because I'm so heavy. If I tread on little creatures like this, it makes me unhappy and then I cry and the tears make my jaw rust up.

Brat comes in with another bucket

Cat How terrible. Now!

The bucket of water goes over the Tinman this time

Tinman That was a sudden shower, I must go indoors.

Cat No shower, my friend!

The Tinman turns with difficulty and sees Brat

Tinman You mean you did it on purpose! I took you for a friend. (*He seizes up*)

Cat And I took you for a ride! Now that you're rusted up let's see what you're made of. (*He opens the door in the Tinman's chest with some difficulty and takes out his heart*) Well, we may be schemers but we're not as heartless as you! Come on, Brat.

Brat looks sadly after the Tinman as he follows Cat off

Dorothy, the Scarecrow and the Lion come in and seeing the Tinman in the distance call out to him

Scarecrow Tinman!
Lion Hello Tinman!
Dorothy Tinman, it's me, Dorothy.

They get to him and realize his plight

Scarecrow He's rusted up.
Dorothy And his heart has been stolen.
Lion What can we do?
Scarecrow Well, the first thing is to get him moving again.
Lion How can we do that?
Scarecrow He keeps an oilcan in his cottage.
Dorothy I'll get it!

   Dorothy goes

Lion Poor Tinman, he was so pleased when the Wizard gave him that heart.
Scarecrow I know. He used to ask me if I'd like to listen to it beating.

   Dorothy comes back with the oilcan

Dorothy Here we are. It seems to be full. Where shall I start?
Scarecrow Oil his jaw first, then he'll be able to tell us what to do next.
Dorothy That's a good idea, I don't know why you need brains, Scarecrow, you seem to do very well without them.

She oils the Tinman's jaw. He opens his mouth with difficulty

Tinman Thank you, friends. Now my neck, please.

Dorothy oils his neck until he can move his head freely

   Now my arms. Thank you. And now my legs. (*He moves his limbs stiffly at first but is soon back to his old self*) I don't know what would have happened if you hadn't come along. I might have stayed here rusting away for ever.
Dorothy I'm glad we got to you in time.
Tinman Dorothy, it's good to see you again. I often think about you. Did you bring Toto with you?
Dorothy Yes, he's here.

They all look at him

Tinman He's just the same as ever. (*Sadly*) And I'm back where I was before, now that my heart has gone.
Dorothy Poor Tinman.
Lion Did you see who took it?
Tinman Yes, it was a gangly boy and a big black cat.
Scarecrow The Witch's cat!
Dorothy It all fits together. The Witch must know that we were coming to see you to ask if you would come with us to her castle.
Tinman But why are you going there?
Dorothy Because the Wicked Witch of the North has stolen the Scarecrow's brains and the Lion's courage.

Tinman I can't believe it.

Scarecrow It's true. I'm more stupid than ever.

Lion And I'm a bigger coward than ever.

Tinman Then we must go to the castle, however dangerous the journey. (*He shuts the door in his chest sadly*) Though I haven't much heart, I'll certainly go with you.

Lion Which way do we go?

Tinman I don't know, there's an old signpost which used to tell the way but it's fallen over.

Dorothy picks it up and turns it round

Dorothy It isn't much help now. It could point anywhere.

Scarecrow I've got an idea. Which way did we come from?

Dorothy (*pointing*) That way.

Scarecrow Then it's easy. We point the arm which says "To Oz" in that direction, then all of the other arms will be right as well.

Dorothy That's right. Aren't you clever? I'd never have thought of that.

Scarecrow (*preening himself*) Oh it's nothing really.

Tinman Let's see then. (*He reads*) "To the Mountains of Darkness". This is the way.

Lion (*shivering*) I don't like the sound of it.

Tinman Don't worry, Lion, we'll look after you. I'll go in front then I can clear any trees away with my axe.

Scarecrow Then Dorothy, then the Lion. I'll hold on to his tail so I don't get lost.

Lion Don't pull it too hard, will you?

Scarecrow Of course not.

Tinman Well, we must start to walk or the sun will have set and we'll have to stay for the night.

Scarecrow (*two tugs on the tail*) Tring, tring. Off we go!

They begin to walk

Dorothy Do you think it's a long way to the Mountains of Darkness, Tinman?

Tinman I don't know. But if you get tired, we'll carry you between us.

Dorothy I don't want to be a burden to you.

Scarecrow Don't worry, the Tinman and I aren't made of flesh and blood like you, so we never get tired.

A flash of light. Music. Glinda, the Good Witch, appears

What was that?

Dorothy Who are you?

Glinda I am Glinda, the Good Witch. I will watch over you and try to help you on your journey.

Dorothy How did you know that we were going on a journey?

Glinda That's easy. I am a witch, but a good witch. Few things are hidden from me.

Scarecrow A good witch? Then why don't you put a spell on the Wicked Witch of the North?

Glinda You don't understand. Her evil powers balance my good ones. I can do nothing without your help. Do you know what a dangerous journey you are undertaking?

Dorothy We know that it won't be easy.

Glinda The Witch's castle is closely guarded. Aren't you afraid?

Lion Yes! That is, not really . . .

Dorothy I'm not afraid as long as I have my friends with me.

Glinda I see you have made up your mind but before you set off, you must put on these shoes.

Dorothy Thank you. I seem to have lost my own.

Scarecrow Aren't they pretty?

Glinda These are no ordinary shoes. They are magic.

Dorothy What can they do?

Glinda You will find out when you need their help. Now I must leave you.

A cymbal clash and she disappears

Lion Ooh! I wish she didn't have to disappear like that!

The Tinman comforts him

Scarecrow Put your new shoes on, Dorothy. Then we can set off.

Dorothy (*putting them on*) They fit perfectly.

Scarecrow They ought to, if they're magic.

Tinman We're all ready? Then off we go!

They march off, we see them silhouetted across the sky and they appear on the other side

Lion I hope the journey isn't too long. I'm getting hungry.

Scarecrow Please Lion, don't go off and kill any animals. You know it upsets the Tinman. Could you try to make do with some nuts and a few berries?

Lion All right. I'll try, but it's no diet for a lion—even a cowardly lion like me.

Tinman Perhaps I wouldn't mind so much if I had a heart but without my heart to guide me I have to be very careful not to hurt anything.

Scarecrow I'm enjoying this walk. Where are we going?

Lion To the Wicked Witch's castle. Use your brains, Scarecrow.

Scarecrow (*sadly*) I haven't got any.

Ugly music

Tinman Listen!

Lion (*nervously*) What's that?

It goes dark suddenly

It's dark. Where is everybody?

Dorothy Don't worry! I'm here, Lion.

Scarecrow There's something funny going on here.

Lion I don't think it's very f-f-f-funny.

Tinman This is no ordinary darkness, it's magic.

The noise stops. Suddenly a strange figure appears in a pool of light

Black Spirit (*in a solemn voice*) Good-evening!

Scarecrow Good-afternoon. Or it was until a moment ago.

Black Spirit Who are you?

Scarecrow I'm a Scarecrow without any brains and these are my friends, the Cowardly Lion, the Tinman, Dorothy and Toto.

Black Spirit Where is Toto?

Dorothy Here in my pinafore pocket, he's very small.

Scarecrow Well, it's nice to have met you. Can we go on now? We've a long journey ahead of us.

Black Spirit Of course. You can go where you please.

Tinman But we can't find our way in this blackness.

Black Spirit That's another matter.

Dorothy But we must. It's very important. Can't you help us?

Black Spirit Why have you come this way?

Dorothy Because we are on our way to the Mountains of Darkness.

Black Spirit And why are you making the journey?

Scarecrow Why are we making the journey? (*He smiles*) That's a good question.

Dorothy We are going to seek out the Wicked Witch of the North.

Scarecrow That's right. The Witch who has stolen my brains.

Lion And stolen my courage.

Tinman And taken away my heart.

Black Spirit Are you sure you know what you're doing? The journey to the Mountains of Darkness is dangerous.

Dorothy We know that, but we have to go. Won't you help us?

Black Spirit I might. If I bring back the light will you do something for me in return?

Dorothy Of course.

Black Spirit In the Witch's castle there are great chests full of treasures that she has stolen but I want something far more valuable.

Dorothy What is it?

Black Spirit When you have captured the Witch you must search until you find a round red box. Inside you will find a black diamond which she stole from me. I will lift the darkness if you promise to bring it to me.

Dorothy That should be quite easy. But why you want a black diamond when you could have all of the other treasures, I can't imagine.

Black Spirit This is no ordinary diamond. Whoever possesses it controls the powers of darkness for ever.

Dorothy We won't forget. And now for your part of the bargain. Will you take away the darkness?

Black Spirit Take this flute. (*He hands it to the Tinman*) Wait until I have completely disappeared, then play it and the light will return.

Dorothy Very well.

Black Spirit And don't forget your promise!

The Black Spirit disappears

Lion He's gone! Oh, Tinman, play the flute quickly. I'm frightened of the dark.

The Tinman plays the flute and the sky brightens

Scarecrow That's better.
Lion Who was he?
Scarecrow I don't know. I'm completely in the dark.
Dorothy Are you all right, Toto?
Scarecrow I don't suppose he minds very much. It must be dark in your pocket all the time.
Dorothy I'll put him down here for a moment. Perhaps he can find some seeds to eat. (*She puts Toto on the ground*) Now don't go far away, Toto. We don't want to have to search for you.
Tinman Before we go any further, could you oil my arms and legs? I'm getting very stiff.
Lion I'll do it. (*He begins to oil the Tinman*)
Scarecrow Shall I take your axe for a moment, Tinman? I'd like to be a woodman. (*He swings the heavy axe over his shoulder and falls over*) Oh dear!
Dorothy (*helping him up*) Are you all right, Scarecrow?
Scarecrow I think so, I fall very softly, you know.

> *Whilst they are occupied, Brat and Cat come in behind them. Suddenly Cat grabs Toto and they rush off*

Tinman Look!

> *The Lion and the others set off after them but although they are nearly caught several times they eventually escape*

Dorothy begins to cry

Lion Don't cry, Dorothy.
Scarecrow Please don't, or you'll make the Tinman cry too.
Dorothy Poor Toto. What will become of him?
Scarecrow I expect they've taken him to the Witch's castle.
Dorothy Then we must hurry on as fast as we can.
Tinman I'm ready.
Scarecrow Then off we go! I like saying that.

They set off. The sky begins to redden

Dorothy The sun is beginning to set. Do you think we'll get there before dark, Tinman?
Tinman I don't know, we'll just have to keep going as long as we can.

A gentle jingling sound

Lion What's that noise?
Scarecrow I don't know, perhaps it's the Tinman's toes.

The sound grows

Lion It's getting louder. I don't like it.
Dorothy Where does it come from?

The jingle becomes a jangle

Scarecrow I don't know, it's more magic I suppose. There's a lot of it about.

The sound becomes uglier

Dorothy It sounds horrible.
Scarecrow I can't hear myself think.

They stop

Tinman It's like a wall of sound. I can't go on.

They all try to pass but the sound makes a barrier which they can't get through

Scarecrow We're stuck.

They all put their hands over their ears. The Scarecrow sees them and puts his hands over his eyes. The music rises to a gruesome crescendo, then stops suddenly

Dorothy (*taking her hands from her ears*) It's stopped.
Scarecrow (*taking his hands from his eyes*) So it has!
Tinman Let's try again.

As soon as he tries to walk on, the music starts again. He stops and the music stops. The wall of sound fascinates the Scarecrow who walks up to it and gives it a poke to which it responds with a single note. He pokes out a tune using his fingers and feet. He stops suddenly when ...

The Music Man appears

The music fades but stays in the background

Music Man Did you want something?
Scarecrow No, not really.
Music Man Who are you?
Scarecrow I am a Scarecrow without any brains and these are my three
    friends, Dorothy, the Cowardly Lion, and the Tinman. There used to be a
    little mouse called Toto as well ...
Music Man Where has he gone?
Lion We're not sure.
Tinman But we've a good idea.
Music Man Now that you are here, what do you want?
Dorothy We want to pass, but the music won't let us.
Music Man (*crossly*) Of course it won't. That's what it's for. It's a wall of
    sound. Took me a long time to make.
Dorothy But we must get through, it's important.
Music Man Where are you going?
Dorothy To the Mountains of Darkness.
Music Man And why are you making the journey?
Scarecrow That's a good question. But I keep forgetting the answer.

Dorothy We're going to seek out the Wicked Witch of the North.

Scarecrow That's right!

Lion Who has stolen my courage.

Tinman And my heart.

Scarecrow And my brains.

Music Man Do you know what a terrible journey it is?

Dorothy We know, but we must go, whatever dangers lie ahead. Won't you help us?

Music Man If I stop my music and let you pass will you do something for me in return?

Dorothy We'll try.

Music Man In the Witch's castle are great rooms full of stolen treasures but take no notice of them. What I want is far more important.

Dorothy What is it?

Music Man When you have captured the Witch you must search for a round red box. Inside you will find——

Tinman A black diamond which belongs to the Black Spirit——

Music Man And a baton which belongs to me.

Scarecrow A bat and what? Does he mean a bat and ball?

Music Man A baton which I need to conduct my music.

Scarecrow (*nonplussed*) I see.

Dorothy That should be quite easy to find. But why you want a baton when you could have all the other treasures I can't imagine.

Music Man This is no ordinary baton. Whoever owns it controls all the sounds in the world.

Dorothy We won't forget. Now for your part of the bargain. Will you silence the music and let us pass?

Music Man When I leave you, the music will start to get louder. Wait until it stops and you will then be free to continue your journey. And don't forget your promise!

The Music Man goes

Scarecrow Shall we go?

Tinman No, we must wait.

Scarecrow (*going up to the wall*) I'll face the music.

The music rises, grows to a crescendo and glides away as the wall dissolves

Lion That's better.

Dorothy We're free again!

Tinman We must be getting near the mountains now. Be careful not to make too much noise.

Scarecrow What will we do when we get there, Tinman?

Tinman We'll hide in the grounds of her castle and plan how to get inside. We'll wait for a good moment and then surprise her.

Scarecrow That sounds exciting!

Dorothy It will soon be night. Do you think we will be able to walk in the light of the moon?

Tinman I think so, the sky looks clear.

Scarecrow I like moonlight. It's so rheumatic.
Lion Romantic!
Scarecrow Yes, I am. (*He dances along happily*)

*Sudden darkness. Then everything turns bright yellow. After a second to blue,
then red, each time the colours change the travellers abruptly change direction*

Lion W-w-w-what's happening?
Tinman I don't know. It's like a maze.
Scarecrow It is. It's amazing all right. It's making me dizzy.
Dorothy But where are we?

A woman in a triangular suit appears

Kay It's very simple, you are inside a kaleidoscope.
Tinman Who are you?
Kay I am Kay, the Queen of the Kaleidoscope.
Dorothy I've got one of those at home but it isn't big enough for people to
    get inside.

Kay holds up her hand. The stage brightens and the colours stop changing

Kay But this is different, this is where we make the rainbows.
Dorothy I thought rainbows were made by sunshine and rain.
Kay If you believe that, you'll believe anything.
Scarecrow I know why it's called a kaleidoscope.
Lion Why, Scarecrow?
Scarecrow Because it makes you collide with everybody.
Lion Oh.
Tinman It's very beautiful but it made us dizzy. Will you please let us free so
    that we can continue our journey?
Kay Where are you going?
Dorothy To the Mountains of Darkness.
Kay And why are you making this journey?
Scarecrow I knew she'd ask that.
Dorothy We are going to seek out the Wicked Witch of the North.
Lion Who has stolen my courage.
Tinman And stolen my heart.
Scarecrow And my brains.
Dorothy And who has stolen Toto, my pet mouse.
Kay You are nearly there. If I allow you to pass through the Kaleidoscope
    will you do something for me in return?
Dorothy We will.
Kay In the Witch's castle are great chests full of treasures. Ignore them.
    What I want is something far more valuable.
Dorothy What is it?
Kay When you have captured the Witch you must search for a round red
    box. Inside you will find——
Tinman A black diamond which belongs to the Black Spirit.
Lion And a baton which belongs to the Music Man.
Kay And a glass prism which was stolen from me.

Dorothy That should be quite easy to find, but why you want a prism when you could have all the treasure, I can't imagine.

Kay This is no ordinary prism. With it I can make rainbows all over the world.

Scarecrow That would be pretty.

Kay Will you bring it to me?

Dorothy We won't forget. Now will you let us go on our way?

Kay Yes. When I have left you, you must stand perfectly still without speaking. The colours will change seven times. When they stop, you will be free to continue your journey. But remember you will be passing through the spectrum ...

Scarecrow That's interesting ...

Kay And if you move before the colours have changed seven times I don't know what ill may befall you. Are you ready?

Tinman Yes.

Kay Remember, keep perfectly still and don't speak until the colours have changed seven times.

Kay goes

The group stands still. After the first colour change, the Scarecrow opens his mouth but the others silence him with a look. After three colour changes, he does it again. At the sixth change he cannot contain himself and jumps for joy

Scarecrow Aren't the colours lovely! Look, oh do look everybody!

Dorothy Oh, Scarecrow!

The colour changes speed up and the travellers are thrown about inside the Kaleidoscope. They are frightened as menacing music builds in time with the light changes. A loud cymbal clash and then sudden darkness

When the Lights come up they are in the Witch's castle. She is waiting for them gleefully

Witch Well, your journey didn't take as long as you expected, did it? Welcome to the Castle of Darkness! (*She laughs*)

The Lights fade

ACT II

We are still in the Witch's castle

Witch Welcome to you all. Welcome to the Cowardly Lion who used to be so brave until I took away his courage.

The Lion roars

Your roaring doesn't scare me. You are in my power. I'll make you have frightening dreams but I'll make your life so miserable that you'll be afraid to wake up. And as for you . . . (*She goes to the Tinman*) You call yourself a Tinman, but without a heart you're no more than a heap of tin cans.

Tinman I know that. That's why I always wanted a heart.

Witch (*with a snarl*) Well, you've seen the last of it! (*She turns to the Scarecrow*) And now we come to the most stupid creature on earth . . .

Scarecrow Oh, hello!

Witch Did you imagine that somebody of my intelligence would be content to be ruled by a brainless wonder like you?

Scarecrow I had some very sharp brains until you stole them!

Dorothy He may not have had any brains but the Scarecrow was a good ruler. All the people of Oz loved him.

Witch Well, we'll see if they still love him when I've knocked all of his stuffing out.

Dorothy (*standing up to her*) You may have us in your power but you won't get away with it. Glinda the Good will see to that.

Witch Oh, you're one of those simple children who thinks that the good always triumph, are you? Well, I'm the last of the Four Wicked Witches of Oz. When they died, their power was handed on to me so I'm four times more powerful than your good witch Glinda will ever be.

Dorothy turns away in despair

Tinman, come here!

He goes to her

You will take off the Scarecrow's crown and polish it until it dazzles. I want it to shine when I'm crowned.

Scarecrow (*to himself*) I'd like to crown her.

Tinman And if I refuse?

Witch Your friend the Lion will suffer.

The Tinman reluctantly takes the crown from the Scarecrow's head

Tinman I'm sorry, Scarecrow.

Scarecrow That's all right. It's rather heavy to wear all the time. When I get my brains back and I'm King again, I think I'll just wear it in bed.

Witch (*sneering*) When you get your brains back! You've a long time to wait!

The Scarecrow is walking round the room trying all of the doors

And you needn't try to get out. These locks were made by a great blacksmith. Only my keys will open them. (*She points to the keys which hang from her waist*) And they're here, where you'll never get them. (*To the Lion*) Now you can get into that cage.

Lion I don't like cages.

Witch Do as I say! Into the cage!

He jumps in and she locks the door

And the rest of you needn't try to get out of the window because you're at the top of a tower and the rocks below are as sharp as needles.

The Witch goes

Scarecrow I'm sorry, everybody.

Tinman What for?

Scarecrow It's my fault. If I had done what the Queen of the Kaleidoscope told us and not moved we wouldn't have got into this trouble.

Dorothy Never mind, Scarecrow. It's done now. No good worrying about what can't be mended.

Scarecrow Thank you, Dorothy.

Dorothy We must put all of our efforts into getting out of here.

Scarecrow And to finding my brains.

Tinman And my heart.

Lion And my courage.

Dorothy And Toto.

Lion I used to think it would be good to live in a zoo without any worries about having to find food or shelter. Now that I see what it's like living behind bars, I know I'd rather be free even if it means going hungry sometimes.

Tinman There's something I don't understand.

Scarecrow What's that?

Tinman Why doesn't she just kill us?

Scarecrow Kill us till we're dead, you mean?

Tinman Yes. She's got all that she wanted. She has taken our most precious possessions. Why does she bother to keep us?

Scarecrow Perhaps one of us has magic powers that she is afraid of.

Tinman I hope you're right, Scarecrow.

Dorothy Listen! Can you hear anything?

Scarecrow Yes, it's something ticking.

Lion Oooh! I don't like the sound of it. (*He shivers with fear, rattling the bars of his cage*)

Dorothy Where is it coming from?

Tinman Over here. It's coming from this chest.

Dorothy Will it open?
Tinman The lid's very heavy.
Scarecrow I'll help.

They tug on the lid which suddenly flies open, hurling the Scarecrow up in the air

Lion Tell me quickly, what is it?

A wizened little old man sits up in the chest. He is wearing an old-fashioned frock coat and sporting a pocket watch as big as an alarm clock

Wizard (*blinking in the light*) Thank you very much. (*He rubs his eyes*) Excuse me, it's very bright after being in the dark so long. (*He climbs out of the chest*)
Scarecrow I'm *still* in the dark. Who are you?
Wizard Don't you remember me? I used to be the Wizard of Oz.
Scarecrow So you were! I didn't expect to see you here.
Wizard Hello, Dorothy!
Dorothy Hello, Wizard.
Wizard And there are my old friends, the Tinman and the Lion.
Tinman Hello, Wizard!
Lion Hello, Wizard. (*He shakes hands through the bars of his cage*) I'm glad to see you.
Dorothy But what are you doing here? We thought you had left the Land of Oz a long time ago when you made the Scarecrow the Ruler of the Emerald City.
Wizard I did. But I didn't get very far. I tried to sail home in a hot-air balloon, but when I was drifting over the Mountains of Darkness, the Wicked Witch of the North sent a flock of evil birds to peck at it. All of the air escaped and when I came down to earth she captured me and then locked me in that chest.
Dorothy Why did she do that?
Wizard She thought I was a real wizard and hoped that she would get some new spells from me. But I'm not a wizard, of course, I'm only a conjurer.
Tinman Are there any other prisoners in the castle?
Wizard Not as far as I know. I haven't seen any other human being for a long time.
Scarecrow It was lucky that we heard your watch ticking.
Wizard Yes. I've managed to keep it going all the time I've been here.
Tinman Can I hear it? (*He listens*) Oh, it's very steady! Just like my heart used to be. It was a lovely heart, Wizard.
Wizard Have you lost it?
Tinman It was stolen from me by the Witch and so was the Lion's courage and the Scarecrow's brains. I suppose you couldn't make us some new ones?
Wizard My dear friends, alas I cannot. I have nothing to make them with. Do you know where she has hidden them?
Tinman No, but we must find them.
Wizard I'll do what I can to help. Now I mustn't let her catch me. I'll come out again when she is asleep.

He gets back into the chest and the Tinman puts down the lid

Dorothy Goodbye, Wizard. We'll open the lid as soon as it's safe.
Scarecrow Look what I've found!
Dorothy What is it?
Scarecrow A big book. It's full of very funny words. I can't read it.
Dorothy It's upside down.
Scarecrow Oh, I'd better stand on my head.
Dorothy No, just turn it up the other way.
Scarecrow That's clever!
Tinman It's a book of spells. Read it out, Scarecrow.
Scarecrow I'm no good at spelling.
Tinman Can you read it, Dorothy?
Dorothy (*reading*) "To turn lead into gold. Take a ton of lead and the tresses of ten fair-haired maidens. To improve the power of a broomstick. Take the eye of a spider."
Tinman We haven't got a broomstick.
Scarecrow Nor the eye of a spider.
Dorothy "To become invisible."
Tinman That sounds more promising.
Dorothy "The wearer of the magic cap shall become invisible to evil persons if he stands on his left leg and recites the following spell:
> Eppe Peppe Kay Kay
> Hillo Hollo Hello
> Zizzy Zuzzy Zik!"
Tinman That's not much use if it only makes you invisible to evil people.
Dorothy Well, the Witch is evil. It's worth a try.
Lion I don't think I'd better try, I can't do much in this cage even if I am invisible.
Dorothy What about you, Tinman?
Tinman I don't think I would be any good. Even if I was invisible I make too much noise. It ought to be the Scarecrow, he's light on his feet.
Scarecrow Yes, that's true. (*He does a little dance to demonstrate and falls over*) Where is it?
Tinman What?
Scarecrow The magic cap.
Dorothy There's an old cap here, try it on, Scarecrow.
Scarecrow Very well. (*He puts on the hat, then stands on his right leg*)
Dorothy Other leg.
Scarecrow What?
Dorothy You have to stand on your left leg.
Scarecrow Oh, I'd better lift my right leg, then. (*He does, and falls over*)
Dorothy Don't lift them both at the same time.
Scarecrow (*getting up*) Stand on my left leg. Right! (*He lifts his right leg*)
> Eppe Peppe Kay Kay
> Hillo Hollo Hello
> Zizzy Zuzzy Zik!

How do I look?
Lion Fine, but you're still visible.

Scarecrow That's because you're good, Lion. I won't be visible to the Witch, you'll see.

Dorothy Here she comes! Are you ready?

The Witch comes in with a broomstick which she throws to Dorothy

Witch Make yourself useful. Sweep the floor.

The Scarecrow goes up to her and whistles in her ear

Ooh! What was that?

He trips her up. She sprawls on the floor

Dorothy The keys! Get the keys.

Witch What's that? Who are you talking to?

The Scarecrow goes to get the keys but as he bends down to get them the hat falls off. The Witch sees him, grabs him by the arm and picks up the cap

Oh, it's you, is it? Too clever by half. Pull me up.

The Scarecrow pulls her up with some difficulty

So you found the secret of the magic cap, did you! Any more tricks from you . . . Do you see what this is? (*She produces a box of matches*) A match! (*She strikes one*)

The Scarecrow is terrified

Now take warning, all of you. Any more of your tricks and the Scarecrow will be the first to suffer.

The Lion roars

Did you say something?

Lion N-n-n-no. I was just yawning.

Witch Have you finished polishing that crown yet?

Tinman Yes. (*He puts it on her throne*)

Witch I told you to sweep the floor!

Dorothy begins to sweep

That's better. (*She sits on her throne but rises with a shriek*) Did you do that on purpose?

Tinman No, I didn't.

Witch I can see I'll have to watch you all more carefully than I thought, but it won't be for long. Tomorrow, my friends, the Winged Monkeys will come, they'll carry you high into the air and drop you into the sea.

Dorothy Why are you doing all this to us? We haven't done you any harm.

Witch You know why. You're good, and that means you're dangerous to me. (*She opens the door to go out*)

Brat, who has been listening at the keyhole, falls into the room

Brat Ooooh!

Witch You useless Brat. What were you doing?

Brat Tying up my shoelace.

Witch Your shoes haven't got laces!

Brat So they haven't.

Witch What a stupid child I've reared. Since you seem so interested in what's going on, you can come in here and guard the prisoners. Make sure that they don't get into mischief during their last few hours on earth.

The Witch goes

The travellers look at Brat with suspicion

Brat Can you keep a secret?

They don't answer

Oh, very well, if you don't want my help . . .

Dorothy Your help? Why should you help us?

Brat Because I don't like her.

Tinman But she's your mother.

Brat So she says, but I think she stole me when I was a baby. She's never behaved like a mother.

Tinman Go on.

Brat And now, I want to escape.

Tinman You've come to the wrong people. We can't escape ourselves.

Brat But you can with my help.

Dorothy How can we trust you when you helped to get us into this mess?

Brat I didn't want to . . . I was only obeying orders.

Dorothy Even when that meant stealing Toto?

Brat Is that your pet mouse?

Dorothy Yes.

Brat I didn't want to steal him. If I tell you where he is, will you believe me then?

Dorothy Is he all right? Yes, I'll believe you. I'll believe anything if you tell me that Toto is safe.

Brat Yes, he's still safe. And he's locked up in that snuff box which she carries all the time.

Tinman How do you know that?

Brat I heard him sneezing this morning.

Dorothy Poor Toto!

Tinman At least it proves he's still alive.

Scarecrow That's true. Now, how can you help us?

Brat My mother tried to teach me lots of magic but I could never get it right. I think my approach was more scientific.

Tinman Go on.

Brat Now although I couldn't do spells, I got interested in herbs and medicines. Last week I made a potion from a recipe I got from an apothecary.

Tinman What?

Brat An apothecary.

Scarecrow Bless you! It's not much fun sneezing. (*Looking at his straw*) I get hay fever sometimes.

Dorothy Scarecrow! Let him get on with his story. We haven't got much time.

Brat This potion is very strong and the old man who gave me the recipe told me that it could make you sleep for a hundred years.

Tinman How does that help us?

Brat Every night, my mother takes a drink which she thinks makes her get younger. I've put my potion into a bottle just like hers. When she comes back, all we have to do is change the bottles and she'll sleep for a hundred years.

Dorothy But we must find out her secrets first. It's no good putting her to sleep if we still can't get out.

Brat The keys round her waist will open all the doors of the castle. What else do you need?

Tinman If we are to get back without breaking our promises we need to find a round red box.

Brat That's easy. It's here. (*He produces it*)

Dorothy (*looking into the box*) He's right. Here is the black diamond, and here is the baton, and here is the prism.

Lion Good, and we know that Toto is in her snuff box.

Tinman Now all we have to do is find out where she has put your courage, the Scarecrow's brains and my heart.

Brat I don't know that. We must trick her into telling us. Will you trust me now?

Tinman Yes. We don't even know your name.

Brat I'm called Brat.

Lion Look out. I can smell the Witch coming!

They all sit down looking as if butter wouldn't melt in their mouths

The Witch unlocks the door and comes in, locking it again behind her

Witch What are you up to? You look too good to be true.

Lion N-n-n-n-n-n-nothing.

Witch You'd better not be. Now, all keep quiet, I want to concentrate. (*She puts the crown over her steeple hat*) It fits me well, I think. Brat!

Brat Yes.

Witch Pour out my potion.

Brat Yes, Mother.

Witch What a polite son you are. Aren't you feeling well?

Brat (*as he changes bottles*) Yes, Mother. I've never felt better.

Witch I'll feel better tomorrow, when this little lot are safely at the bottom of the sea.

Brat Then will you use the brains and courage and heart to make a spell?

Witch No, they're useless except to their owners and they won't be needing them any more.

Brat I expect you've kept them in a safe place.

Witch No, they're no longer important, now that they have become my prisoners. I've got them here, in my hat.

Brat In your hat?

The travellers register this information

Witch Yes. When the Winged Monkeys drop these silly people into the sea tomorrow, they can drop my hat after them. I won't need it when I'm wearing the crown of Oz.

Brat (*flattering her*) Oh, what a clever witch you are!

Witch Yes, I am, aren't I? And I'm getting younger and cleverer every day. If I drink my magic potion regularly, I shall live for ever.

Scarecrow What a nasty thought!

Witch What was that?

Scarecrow I said "so you ought".

Witch It's been a long day. (*She drinks*) But tomorrow I'll be Queen and with this (*she drinks some more*) I shall be Queen for ever. (*She begins to doze*)

Brat Oh no you won't! You thought I was stupid, but you've drunk the wrong potion. Something that I concocted.

She tries to struggle to her feet

You won't get younger, you'll get older like everybody else—but not until you have slept for a hundred years.

Witch You scoundrel! I wondered why you were being so polite to me. (*She collapses and falls into a deep sleep*)

Scarecrow Night night!

Tinman You've done it, Brat!

Dorothy Good. Now we must act quickly; we've a lot of things to remember, Tinman.

Tinman Yes, Dorothy.

Dorothy Will you get the things from the red box?

Tinman Yes, they're all here. (*He collects the diamond, baton and prism*)

Dorothy And Scarecrow, will you open the chest so that the Wizard can get out?

Scarecrow Yes. (*He tries in vain*) It's too heavy for me.

Lion I'll help if you'll unlock the cage, Scarecrow.

Scarecrow That's a good idea. Here you are. (*He unlocks the cage with the key which he takes from the Witch's belt*)

Lion Thank you. That's an experience I don't want again in a hurry. (*He helps the Scarecrow with the lid*)

Scarecrow Wizard! It's all right, you can come out.

The Wizard sits up

Wizard Are you sure?

Scarecrow Yes, she's asleep for a very long time.

Wizard That's good. Perhaps we'll all get some peace now. (*He gets out of the chest and stretches himself*) I can hardly believe that I'm back in the world again. I thought I would have to remain in that trunk until the end of my days.

Tinman What will you do now, Wizard? Would you like to come back to the Emerald City with us?

Wizard No, thank you my friends. I have had enough adventures for the time being. As soon as we get away from here I'm going home to join a circus again.

Scarecrow Isn't it a long way?

Wizard Yes, but it's all downhill.

Brat I've always wanted to join a circus. Can I come with you, Wizard?

Wizard I expect so, I'll be pleased to have a companion on the journey.

Brat Hurrah! (*He pretends to juggle. Maybe turns a cartwheel*)

Dorothy (*very practical*) Will you bring the Witch's hat, Wizard?

Wizard Why do you need that?

Dorothy It has some very precious things inside.

Scarecrow The brains that you gave me.

Lion And the courage that you gave me.

Tinman And the heart that you gave me.

The Wizard removes the Witch's hat and puts it on his own head

Wizard Is there anything else?

Dorothy Yes, something that's very precious to me.

Wizard What's that?

Dorothy The snuff box.

Wizard I didn't know you took snuff.

Dorothy I don't. (*She takes the snuff box from the sleeping Witch*)

Scarecrow Open it, Dorothy.

She can't bring herself to open it

Tinman Shall I open it for you?

Dorothy Yes please, Tinman. (*She gives him the box*)

Tinman (*opening it*) It's all right, he's quite safe.

Dorothy (*taking the mouse from the box*) Oh, Toto, it's good to have you back. I'll never let you out of my sight again.

Scarecrow What does snuff smell like? (*He takes a big sniff*) Atishoo! That's funny, it's given me a bad cold.

Tinman Are we all ready?

Lion Yes, and roaring to go.

Tinman It's nearly dawn, so we should be able to see all right.

Dorothy takes the key, opens the door and they all go out. The Scarecrow reappears suddenly

Scarecrow I nearly forgot! Good-night, Wicked old Witch of the North. I hope you enjoy your long, long sleep. (*He takes the crown*) I don't suppose you'll be needing this any more. Sweet dreams!

He puts the crown over his battered old hat and follows the others

The dawn begins to break. In the distance a cock crows. The Witch twitches once or twice then slowly wakes up and takes in the scene

Witch They've gone! Yes, now I remember! That Brat said he'd given me a potion to put me to sleep for a hundred years, but he got it wrong as usual. He forgot my magic cockerel. His crowing has broken the spell. (*She rises*) So watch out, little travellers, I haven't finished with you yet!

The Lights fade. When they come up again we see the travellers at the parting of the ways

Wizard This is the crossroad, friends. My new companion and I will leave you here. We must travel south and the Emerald City lies that way. But before I go, there is something I must do. Scarecrow!

Scarecrow Yes, Wizard.

Wizard (*removing the Witch's hat*) Here are your brains again. Don't forget to use them wisely. And keep them polished so they don't get rusty.

Scarecrow Yes, I will. (*He puts the brains under his hat, pricking his finger as he does so*) Just as sharp as ever!

Wizard And Tinman . . .

Tinman Yes, Wizard?

Wizard Here is your heart. (*He takes it from the hat*)

Tinman Isn't it fine?

Wizard Still as good as new. (*He opens the Tinman's chest and puts the heart in place*)

Tinman Thank you. I'll try to look after it better this time.

Wizard And Lion . . .

Lion Yes, Wizard.

Wizard This is what you want, I think. (*He produces the bottle*)

The Lion takes a swig

How do you feel?

Lion Full of courage! (*He roars and beats his chest*)

Wizard And now, we must be on our way.

Scarecrow (*rubbing his eyes with his sleeve*) It makes me sad to see you go.

Wizard Now then, be brave like the Lion. Dry your eyes.

Scarecrow I haven't got a hanky.

Wizard Here you are. (*He fishes into the Scarecrow's pocket and pulls out a long multicoloured silk handkerchief*)

All Goodbye, Wizard.

Brat Goodbye, everybody!

Dorothy Goodbye, Brat, thank you for helping us.

Suddenly the Cat rushes in

They are all apprehensive but he soon dispels their fears

Cat Brat, I've been listening to everything. Now that the Witch is asleep, I'm free. Can I come with you?

Brat Do you know that I'm going to join the circus?

Cat Yes. I thought we might do some clowning together.

Brat (*after a moment's thought*) All right, but you'll have to behave yourself. Come on, the Wizard's waiting!

They go off together

Scarecrow Goodbye. (*He waves a sad farewell*)

Tinman It's still a long way back to the Emerald City, I'm afraid.

They set off

Lion Are you? I'm not afraid of anything any more.
Dorothy Cheer up, Scarecrow, you've got your brains back and you'll soon be home.
Scarecrow You're right. Can I listen to your heart, Tinman?
Tinman Come here then.
Scarecrow (*listening*) It has a good steady beat.
Tinman Yes. It's good to have it back again.

They walk on. Suddenly everything goes dark and then the bright colours start again; they are back inside the Kaleidoscope, and begin to change directions rapidly as they did before

I hope that this won't go on for too long. It doesn't do my joints any good at all.

As the light brightens, Kay appears

Kay I didn't expect you back so soon. Did you get to the Witch's castle?
Tinman Yes, quicker than we expected!
Kay And you got inside?
Tinman Yes.
Kay And you found the red box?
Tinman Yes.
Kay And you remembered your promise?
Tinman Yes.
Kay Then if you will give me the prism I will let you pass.
Tinman (*handing it to her*) There you are.
Kay Thank you. I am grateful to you. (*She holds the prism up to the light and fills the sky with brilliant patterns*)
Scarecrow Isn't that pretty!
Kay Now for my part of the bargain. Do you remember what you have to do?

They all look at the Scarecrow

Scarecrow Yes. Wait until the colours change seven times without moving or speaking.
Kay And you won't forget this time?
Scarecrow Of course not. Do you think I haven't got any brains?
Kay Very well.

Kay goes

They stand still, the Lights dim and the colours change through the spectrum. The Scarecrow nearly speaks, but remembers just in time. The Lights brighten again and they are free to walk on

Lion That's a funny business. Very clever.
Scarecrow Oh, there's nothing to it really.
Tinman It's getting very hot.

Scarecrow (*touching Tinman's arm*) I can't tell the difference between hot and cold.

Dorothy (*touching Tinman's other arm*) You're very hot, Tinman. Should we rest in the shade for a while?

Lion That's a good idea. I'll hold the box for you, Tinman.

Tinman Thank you, Lion. (*He hands it over and sits down*)

Dorothy sits next to him

Dorothy I'm getting very hungry.

Scarecrow I never get hungry but I'll go and see if I can find some blackberries for you.

The Scarecrow goes off

The Lion puts the box down beside him, lies on his back, kicks his legs in the air for a few moments and is soon asleep

Dorothy Tinman, do you need oiling?

Tinman No, thank you. I'm feeling very well now that I'm in the shade. It isn't an easy life being a Tinman, when the sun shines I get too hot and when it rains I get rusty.

Dorothy It must be difficult.

Tinman But as long as I have my heart, I am well content.

Whilst they are talking the Witch creeps in and grabs the box. She rushes off cackling with glee

Dorothy and the Tinman do not see her

Dorothy What was that?

Tinman I don't know, some wild bird, I expect.

Dorothy I've never heard a bird like that before.

Lion (*waking suddenly*) Where am I?

Tinman There's nothing to be afraid of, Lion. You've been asleep, that's all.

Lion I had a horrible dream. I thought that the Witch came back and stole the red box. I'm glad to be awake again.

Tinman Where is it?

Lion What?

Tinman The box.

Lion You had it.

Tinman No, I gave it to you.

Lion That's right, so you did. I put it down here!

Dorothy Are you sure?

Lion Positive.

Dorothy Then somebody must have taken it.

The Scarecrow rushes in

Scarecrow Do you know who I've just seen?

Dorothy Who?

Scarecrow The Witch.

Dorothy That's impossible.

Scarecrow I'm sure it was her.

Dorothy But she's supposed to stay asleep for a hundred years.

Scarecrow She must have found an anecdote.

Tinman Antidote!

Scarecrow Yes. She must have had some magic power that we didn't know about.

Dorothy Now what shall we do? The Music Man won't let us pass unless we give him the baton.

Tinman Well, we can't go back so we must go forward. We'll tell the Music Man what happened and ask if he will release us from our promise.

Lion I'm sorry, Dorothy. I should have been more careful.

Dorothy It wasn't your fault, Lion. I thought we were safe. I should have known better.

Tinman Listen!

The jingle begins

Scarecrow We must be nearly there.

Dorothy It's very frightening.

The jingle becomes a jangle and they are held by it

Lion Let's hope he'll be kind.

A crescendo. It stops

The Music Man appears from the shadows

Music Man So you're back. Did you get to the Witch's castle?

Dorothy Yes.

Music Man And you found the box?

Lion Yes.

Music Man And you remembered your promise?

Tinman Yes.

Music Man And you took the baton?

Scarecrow Yes.

Music Man Then if you give it to me, I will let you pass.

Scarecrow I'm sorry, I can't.

Music Man You can't? Do you mean you won't?

Scarecrow No. I can't. When I said yes, I meant no. You see, we did take the baton but on the way here it was stolen from us.

Music Man Then I'm afraid you have broken your promise and I can't let you pass.

Scarecrow (*to the others*) What do we do now?

Lion I could roar and frighten him, I suppose.

Tinman No. A promise is a promise.

Scarecrow I've got an idea! Let's call the Queen of the Fieldmice. She may be able to help us.

Dorothy Have you still got the whistle, Tinman?

Tinman Yes.

Scarecrow Then blow it as hard as you can.

The Tinman blows the whistle

  The Fieldmouse hurries in

Fieldmouse I think I can guess what you want. It's this, isn't it? (*She produces the baton*)
Dorothy (*amazed*) Yes. However did you get it?
Fieldmouse I was at the edge of the wood and saw the Witch steal the red box from you. She rushed off so excited that she didn't notice that the lid wasn't fastened. The baton fell out and some of my subjects found it and brought it to me.
Lion That's wonderful! To think that tiny little creatures like mice can be so clever.
Dorothy We are very grateful. We'll never be able to repay you.
Fieldmouse Perhaps you can help me again one day. Goodbye.

  She goes

Dorothy Goodbye!
Scarecrow Here you are, Music Man, we have kept our promise after all.
Music Man Thank you. (*He takes the baton*) And now I shall keep my part of the bargain.

He conducts the music which has remained in the background. The discords give way to a melody which rises to a peak and then dies away

  The Music Man exits

The travellers discover that they can walk freely again. They go on

Tinman I'm glad that the Music Man got his baton. His music sounds much sweeter now.
Scarecrow Yes, he was very crotchety without it!
Lion Oooh!
Dorothy I expect we will be meeting the Black Spirit soon, Lion. Would you like me to hold your hand?
Lion No, thank you Dorothy. I won't be nervous this time. There's nothing to be afraid of in the dark.
Tinman There's only one problem. We haven't got the black diamond and without that the Black Spirit won't let us pass.
Scarecrow The Fieldmouse helped us last time. Perhaps something will turn up.
Lion Have you noticed, it's getting darker.
Scarecrow So it is.

It gets very dark. They stop

  The Black Spirit appears out of the darkness

Black Spirit So you're back. Did you get to the Witch's castle?
Dorothy Yes.
Black Spirit And you found the box?
Lion Yes.

Black Spirit And you remembered your promise?

Tinman Yes.

Black Spirit And you took the black diamond?

Scarecrow Yes.

Black Spirit Then if you give it to me, I will let you pass.

Scarecrow I'm sorry, I can't.

Black Spirit You can't? Do you mean you won't?

Scarecrow No. I can't. When I said yes, I meant no. You see we did take the black diamond but on our way here it was stolen from us.

Black Spirit Then I'm afraid you have broken your promise and I cannot let you pass.

Scarecrow (*to the others*) What do we do this time?

Tinman Would you accept something else instead?

Black Spirit What have you got that could be equal to the black diamond?

Tinman There's only one thing that I know of. (*He opens his chest*) It's my heart. It may not have magic powers but it's the best thing I have. (*He is about to hand it to the Black Spirit*)

Dorothy Tinman! You can't do that. You mustn't. (*She takes it from him*)

Tinman What else can we do?

The Witch appears from nowhere

Witch I'll tell you what you can do. You can turn round and start walking back to the Mountains of Darkness. I have the black diamond and without it you will never get to the Emerald City. Tonight the Winged Monkeys will carry you into the sky and drop you into the deepest ocean where you will all perish.

Scarecrow If only we had one magic wish.

Witch (*mocking*) And what would you wish?

Dorothy I know what I would wish. (*She stamps her foot*) I would wish that you would start to spin like a top. (*She stamps again*) That the wind would lift you into the sky (*she stamps for the third time*) and that it would drop you into the bottom of the sea where you would stay for ever!

Witch (*in horror*) The shoes! The magic shoes!

The sound of a whirlwind

How did you know the power of the magic shoes? (*She begins to spin round*) Ooooh!

She spins faster and faster and disappears with a loud scream which dies away as she is blown into the air

The travellers are overjoyed, but can hardly believe their good fortune

Dorothy What did she mean about the magic shoes?

Scarecrow I don't know, perhaps she means that the shoes are magic.

Lion Then why didn't the Witch disappear before?

Tinman I don't know.

A sound of sweet music and the Good Witch Glinda appears

Glinda Then I will tell you. When the wearer of the shoes stamps three times the winds obey her command.

Scarecrow That's very extraordinary.

Glinda That's the last anybody will see of the Wicked Witch of the North.

Tinman And look what she left behind! (*He picks up the black diamond*)

Lion The black diamond. I'm glad she didn't take that to the bottom of the sea with her.

Dorothy (*to the Black Spirit*) Now that we are able to keep our promise, will you bring back the light so that we can go on our way?

Black Spirit Of course. Have you still got the flute?

Tinman Yes.

Black Spirit Then you know what to do.

The Black Spirit goes

Scarecrow Play it, Tinman.

The Tinman plays, the sky brightens

What a very pretty tune. Will you play it as we walk home?

Lion If the magic shoes worked before, perhaps they will take us back to the Emerald City.

Dorothy Do you think they will?

Glinda smiles

Scarecrow Try it, Dorothy, but be careful what you tell the winds to do. I don't want to join the Witch at the bottom of the sea. I hate it when my straw gets wet.

Dorothy Lift the Scarecrow and the Lion and the Tinman gently and take them to the Emerald City! (*She stamps her foot three times*)

The winds lift them into the air

Tinman Dorothy, don't forget yourself!

Dorothy Oh yes. And take me with them! (*She floats into the air with them*)

Glinda Goodbye!

All Goodbye!

Glinda disappears

The sky turns from blue to green as they approach the Emerald City

Tinman And here we are, home again.

Scarecrow We seem to be coming back much quicker than we went.

They land on earth again

Lion It's extraordinary how a wind can be strong enough to lift a mighty beast like me way above the clouds.

Scarecrow I enjoyed the ride. (*He starts to spin round*) I wish we could do it all over again.

Lion Scarecrow! Remember where you are. Now that you are back in your own kingdom you must behave with dignity.

Scarecrow Must I? I'll do my best. (*He tries to walk in a dignified manner but trips over*) I don't think I'll ever manage it. Now that we're back safe and sound would you like to come to my palace for dinner?

Tinman It's very kind of you to offer, Scarecrow, but I never need any food and I think I ought to go back to my cottage. I've a lot of logs to chop before the winter.

Lion And I think I ought to go back to the jungle. I want to practise some roaring now that I've got my courage back.

Dorothy I'd like to come with you, Scarecrow, but I've been away from home for a long time and I'm sure my uncle and auntie will be worrying about me.

Scarecrow (*bravely*) Oh well, it's a lonely business being a king.

Dorothy I hope that my magic shoes will take me. I'm going to command the winds to carry me there at once. (*She throws her arms round the Lion*) Goodbye, Lion.

Lion I hope you won't forget me, Dorothy.

Dorothy No, never. (*She hugs the Tinman*) Goodbye, Tinman. Now then, you mustn't cry, you know it makes you rusty.

Tinman Goodbye, Dorothy.

Dorothy (*Kissing the Scarecrow*) Goodbye, Scarecrow. Think about me sometimes.

Scarecrow Yes, I will. (*Sadly*) Goodbye.

Dorothy Goodbye, everybody. (*She wipes away a tear*) Mighty winds, I've had some wonderful adventures in the Land of Oz but I want to see my Uncle Henry and Aunt Em. Take me home again! (*She stamps her foot three times*)

There is a rushing wind which spins everybody round. Dorothy is in the centre and the others move in a circle round her

As they spin faster they drift off into the darkness, until . . .

The little girl is left spinning alone in the centre. The wind dies with the Lights. When the sun rises, Dorothy is lying in the garden

Dorothy I can't believe it. There's the house and the cowsheds and the barn. I'm home again. Uncle Henry!

Uncle Henry enters

Henry Who is it?

Dorothy Don't you see, it's me, Dorothy.

Henry (*putting on his specs*) Bless my soul, so it is. I can hardly believe it. Em!

Em (*off*) Whatever is the matter?

Em comes in

Why Dorothy! (*She hugs her*) I didn't think you would ever come back. Where have you been?

Dorothy Well, you remember the cyclone?

Em Remember it! We've only just finished repairing the roof of the barn.

Dorothy Well, it blew me away to the Emerald City again. And I met the

Tinman and the Cowardly Lion and the Scarecrow just like I did before. Only this time there was a Wicked Witch.

Em A wicked witch. (*Smiling*) I wonder what you'll be dreaming up next.

Dorothy It wasn't a dream. (*Her excitement carries her on*) I know it wasn't.

Henry The things you think of, child!

Dorothy I didn't just think of them, Uncle Henry, they really happened.

Henry Well, I'll just lock the chickens up for the night and then you can tell me all about it.

He goes off

Em And I'll get you a good hot supper ready. I'm pleased that you're back again, child.

Dorothy (*hugging her*) Oh Aunt Em, it's lovely to go on adventurous journeys—but isn't it good to be home again!

Aunt Em goes into the house

(*Talking to herself*) They don't believe I had all those adventures. They think I've been dreaming, but I know I wasn't. I'll never be able to make them believe me. (*She begins to have doubts*) Was I only dreaming? (*She looks down*) Of course, my magic shoes! Now I'm sure it wasn't a dream.

She dances away as the play ends

FURNITURE AND PROPERTY LIST

ACT I

The farm

On stage: Table. *On it:* lamp, knife for **Henry**, knitting for **Em**
2 chairs
Trapdoor to cellar

Personal: **Dorothy**: pet mouse in pocket (required for most scenes)

The gates of the Palace of Oz

On stage: Ornamental gates
Green throne behind gates

Personal: **Fieldmouse**: whistle
Scarecrow: crown on top of hat (required for most scenes)

Clearing in the wood

Personal: **Lion**: bottle

Witch's castle

On stage: Steaming cauldron

Off stage: Bottle (**Brat**)

The edge of the wood

On stage: Signpost with various arms, on ground

Off stage: Bucket of water (**Brat**)
Bucket of water (**Brat**)
Oilcan (**Dorothy**)
Shoes (**Glinda**)
Flute (**Black Spirit**)

Personal: **Tinman**: axe, heart inside chest (required for most scenes)

Witch's castle

On stage: Cauldron
Throne
Cage
Chest
Book of spells
Cap
Round red box containing black diamond, baton, prism
Key in door
Potion bottle, cup

ACT II

Witch's castle

On stage: As end Act I

Off stage: Broomstick **(Witch)**

Personal: **Scarecrow**: crown
Witch: bunch of keys on belt, box of matches, snuff box containing Toto
Wizard: large pocket watch
Brat: potion bottle

Crossroads and journey

On stage: Signpost

Off stage: Baton **(Fieldmouse)**
Black diamond **(Witch)**
Red box containing prism, baton, black diamond **(Tinman)**

Personal: **Wizard**: Witch's hat containing brains, heart, bottle
Scarecrow: crown, multicoloured silk handkerchief
Tinman: whistle, flute

The farm

Off stage: Spectacles **(Henry)**

LIGHTING PLOT

Various simple settings on an open stage

ACT I

To open: Lighting on **Em** and **Henry** at table

Cue 1	**Em** (*worried*): "I don't like it at all." *Decrease lighting*	(Page 2)
Cue 2	**Dorothy**: "Here we go again." *Crack of lightning, continue to decrease lighting to black-out*	(Page 3)
Cue 3	When ready *Bring up lighting on gates to Palace of Oz with green background sky lighting*	(Page 3)
Cue 4	**Dorothy** and **Scarecrow** go off *Fade to black-out*	(Page 7)
Cue 5	When ready *Bring up lighting on Witch*	(Page 7)
Cue 6	**Witch** chuckles with glee *Fade to black-out*	(Page 8)
Cue 7	When ready *Bring up lighting on clearing in woods*	(Page 8)
Cue 8	**Dorothy**: ". . . I'll hold your hand." *Fade to black-out*	(Page 10)
Cue 9	When ready *Bring up lighting on* **Witch**, *with light under cauldron*	(Page 10)
Cue 10	**Witch**: ". . . will be mine!" *Cauldron flares brightly for a minute, then fade to black-out*	(Page 11)
Cue 11	When ready *Bring up lighting at edge of wood*	(Page 11)
Cue 12	**Dorothy**, **Tinman**, **Scarecrow** and **Lion** march off *Light to silhouette them against the sky*	(Page 14)
Cue 13	**Lion** (*nervously*): "What's that?" *Partial black-out*	(Page 15)
Cue 14	**Tinman**: ". . . it's magic." *Pool of light on* **Black Spirit**	(Page 16)
Cue 15	**Black Spirit** disappears *Cut pool of light*	(Page 17)

Cue 16	**Tinman** plays flute *Increase lighting*	(Page 17)
Cue 17	**Dorothy**, **Scarecrow**, **Tinman** and **Lion** set off *Change to red background lighting, as sun sets*	(Page 17)
Cue 18	**Scarecrow**: "Yes, I am." (*He dances along happily*) *Black-out, then snap up yellow lighting, then blue, then red—* *continue changing*	(Page 20)
Cue 19	**Kay** holds up her hand *Increase general lighting; stop colours changing*	(Page 20)
Cue 20	**Kay** goes *Begin colour changes*	(Page 21)
Cue 21	**Dorothy**: "Oh, Scarecrow!" *Colour changes speed up—continue for a short while, then sud-* *den black-out*	(Page 21)
Cue 23	When ready *Snap up lighting on Witch's castle*	(Page 21)
Cue 24	**Witch** laughs *Fade to black-out*	(Page 21)

ACT II

To open:	Lighting on Witch's castle	
Cue 25	**Scarecrow** follows the others off *Dawn lighting*	(Page 30)
Cue 26	**Witch**: "... finished with you yet!" *Fade to black-out*	(Page 31)
Cue 27	When ready *Bring up lighting on crossroads*	(Page 31)
Cue 28	**Tinman**: "... have it back again." They walk on *Repeat Cue 18*	(Page 32)
Cue 29	**Tinman**: "... any good at all." *Repeat Cue 19*	(Page 32)
Cue 30	**Kay** holds prism up to the light *Brilliant coloured patterns on sky*	(Page 32)
Cue 31	**Kay** goes *Dim lights, then different coloured lights as before, then return* *to bright general lighting*	(Page 32)
Cue 32	**Lion**: "... in the dark." *Decrease lighting gradually*	(Page 35)
Cue 33	**Scarecrow**: "So it is." *Partial black-out*	(Page 35)
Cue 34	**Tinman** plays flute *Increase lighting, with blue sky background*	(Page 37)

| *Cue* 35 | **Glinda** disappears | (Page 37) |
| | *Change to green sky background* | |

| *Cue* 36 | As they spin faster | (Page 38) |
| | *Dim lighting* | |

| *Cue* 37 | **Dorothy** is left spinning alone | (Page 38) |
| | *Black-out* | |

| *Cue* 38 | When ready | (Page 38) |
| | *Bring up general lighting on farm* | |

EFFECTS PLOT

Note: Many of the effects listed below may be performed live by a percussionist—see Author's Note on page iv.

ACT I

Cue 1	**Em** (*worried*): "I don't like it at all." *Clap of thunder, sudden rush of wind*	(Page 2)
Cue 2	**Dorothy**: "... I can't go without you." *Wind rises to a crescendo*	(Page 2)
Cue 3	**Dorothy**: "Here we go again." *Crash of thunder*	(Page 3)
Cue 4	Black-out *Strange music—fade as lights come up*	(Page 3)
Cue 5	**Dorothy**: "Thank you." *Cymbal crash*	(Page 4)
Cue 6	**Scarecrow** taps his head *Solid knocking sound*	(Page 5)
Cue 7	Lights fade to black-out *Eerie music—fade as lights come up*	(Page 7)
Cue 8	As lights come up on **Witch** *Steam from cauldron*	(Page 10)
Cue 9	**Witch**: "... will be mine!" *Cauldron belches steam*	(Page 11)
Cue 10	**Scarecrow**: "... so we never get tired." *Flash, music as **Glinda** appears*	(Page 14)
Cue 11	**Glinda**: "Now I must leave you." *Cymbal clash*	(Page 15)
Cue 12	**Scarecrow** (*sadly*): "I haven't got any." *Ugly music*	(Page 15)
Cue 13	**Tinman**: "... it's magic." *Cut music*	(Page 16)
Cue 14	**Tinman**: "... as long as we can." *Gentle jingling sound*	(Page 17)
Cue 15	**Scarecrow**: "... the Tinman's toes." *Increase sound*	(Page 17)
Cue 16	**Dorothy**: "Where does it come from?" *Change to jangling sound, becoming uglier and louder*	(Page 18)

| *Cue* 17 | **Scarecrow** puts hands over his eyes | (Page 18) |
| | *Music rises to gruesome crescendo then stops suddenly* | |

| *Cue* 18 | As **Scarecrow** pokes wall of sound | (Page 18) |
| | *Single note each time he pokes* | |

| *Cue* 19 | **Music Man** appears | (Page 18) |
| | *Fade music to background level* | |

| *Cue* 20 | **Music Man** goes | (Page 19) |
| | *Increase music to a crescendo, then let it glide away* | |

| *Cue* 21 | As colour changes speed up | (Page 21) |
| | *Menacing music, building in time with the light changes—continue for a short while, then loud cymbal clash to coincide with sudden black-out* | |

ACT II

| *Cue* 22 | **Tinman**: "I hope you're right, Scarecrow." | (Page 23) |
| | *Ticking noise* | |

| *Cue* 23 | **Wizard** climbs out of the chest | (Page 24) |
| | *Fade ticking* | |

| *Cue* 24 | **Scarecrow** follows the others off; dawn begins to break | (Page 30) |
| | *Cock crows in distance* | |

| *Cue* 25 | **Tinman**: "Listen!" | (Page 34) |
| | *Jingling noise* | |

| *Cue* 26 | **Dorothy**: "It's very frightening." | (Page 34) |
| | *Jingle becomes a jangle, growing to a crescendo then stopping suddenly* | |

| *Cue* 27 | **Music Man** appears from shadows | (Page 34) |
| | *Bring up discordant music quietly as background* | |

| *Cue* 28 | **Music Man** conducts music | (Page 35) |
| | *Discords give way to melody, which rises to a peak then dies away* | |

| *Cue* 29 | **Witch**: "The magic shoes!" | (Page 36) |
| | *Sounds of a whirlwind—continue until **Witch** disappears* | |

| *Cue* 30 | **Tinman**: "I don't know." | (Page 36) |
| | *Sweet music as **Glinda** appears* | |

| *Cue* 31 | **Dorothy** stamps her foot three times | (Page 37) |
| | *Sound of gentle winds* | |

| *Cue* 32 | They land on earth again | (Page 37) |
| | *Fade winds* | |

| *Cue* 33 | **Dorothy** stamps her foot three times | (Page 38) |
| | *Rushing wind* | |

| *Cue* 34 | Black-out | (Page 38) |
| | *Fade wind* | |

MADE AND PRINTED IN GREAT BRITAIN BY
LATIMER TREND & COMPANY LTD PLYMOUTH
MADE IN ENGLAND